The Complete Anti-Stress Colouring Collection Book 5

by Christina Rose

The ultimate calming colouring book collection

The Complete Anti-stress Colouring Collection Book 5
The ultimate calming colouring book collection

First published in the United Kingdom in 2015 by
Bell & Mackenzie Publishing Limited

ISBN:978-1-910771-61-7

A CIP catalogue record of this book is available from the British Library

Created by Christina Rose

Contributors: under licence from shutterstock
www.bellmackenzie.com

Show me your hands. Do they have scars from giving? Show me your feet. Are they wounded in service? Show me your heart. Have you left a place for divine love?

Fulton J. Sheen

Be faithful to that which exists within yourself.

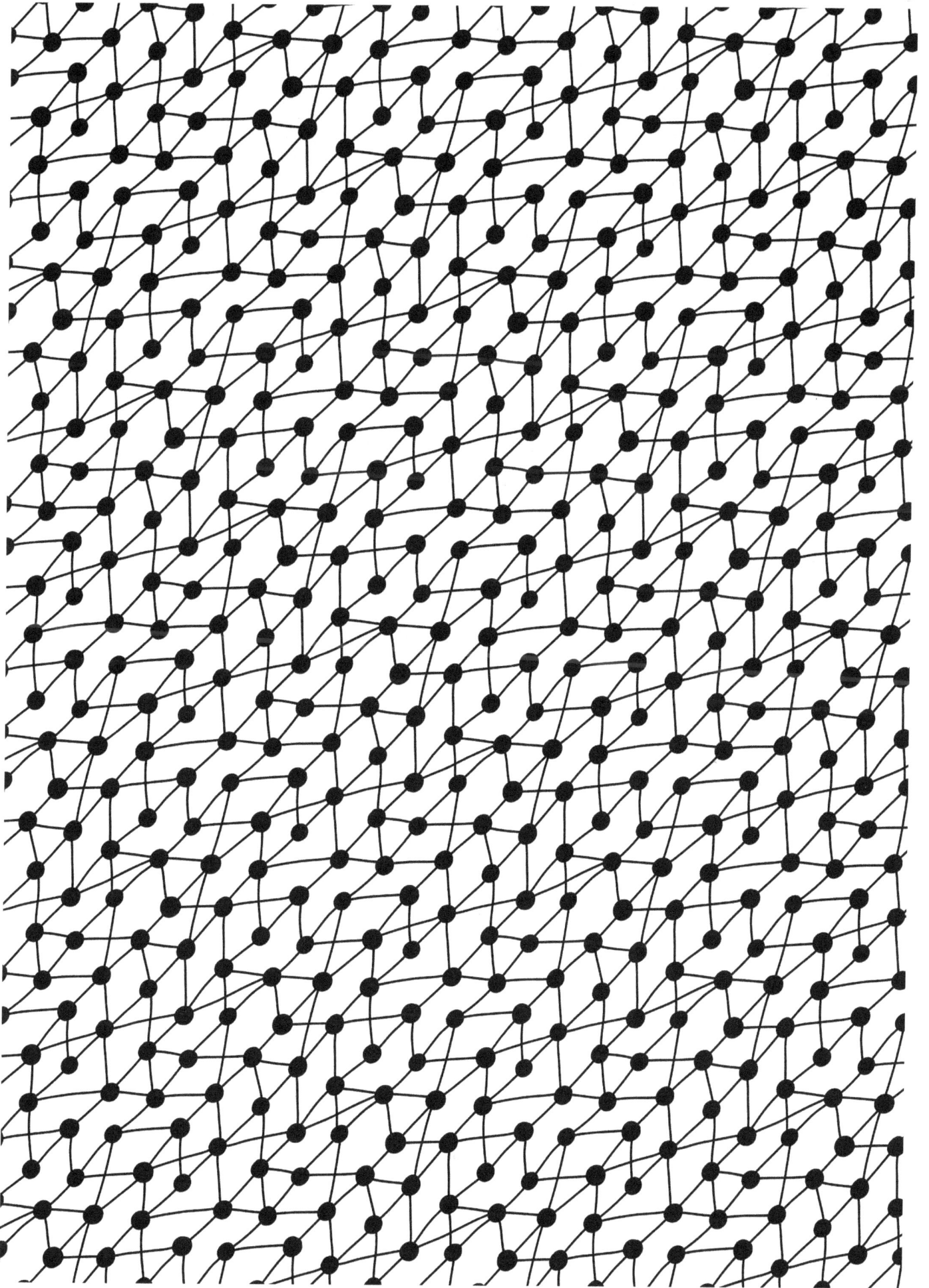

Tears are often the telescope by which men see far into heaven.

Happiness is not something you postpone for the future; it is something you design for the present.

Jim Rohn

All you need is the plan, the road map, and the courage to press on to your destination.

Earl Nightingale

What makes the desert beautiful is
that somewhere it hides a well.

Antoine de Saint-Exupery

If you accept the expectations of others, especially negative ones, then you never will change the outcome.

Author unknown

You are always free to change your mind and choose a different future, or a different past.

Richard Bach

There is a loftier ambition than merely to stand high in the world. It is to stoop down and lift mankind a little higher.

Author unknown

Only those who have learned the power of sincere and selfless contribution experience life's deepest joy: true fulfillment.

Tony Robbins

Be brave enough to live life creatively. The creative place where no one else has ever been.

Alan Alda

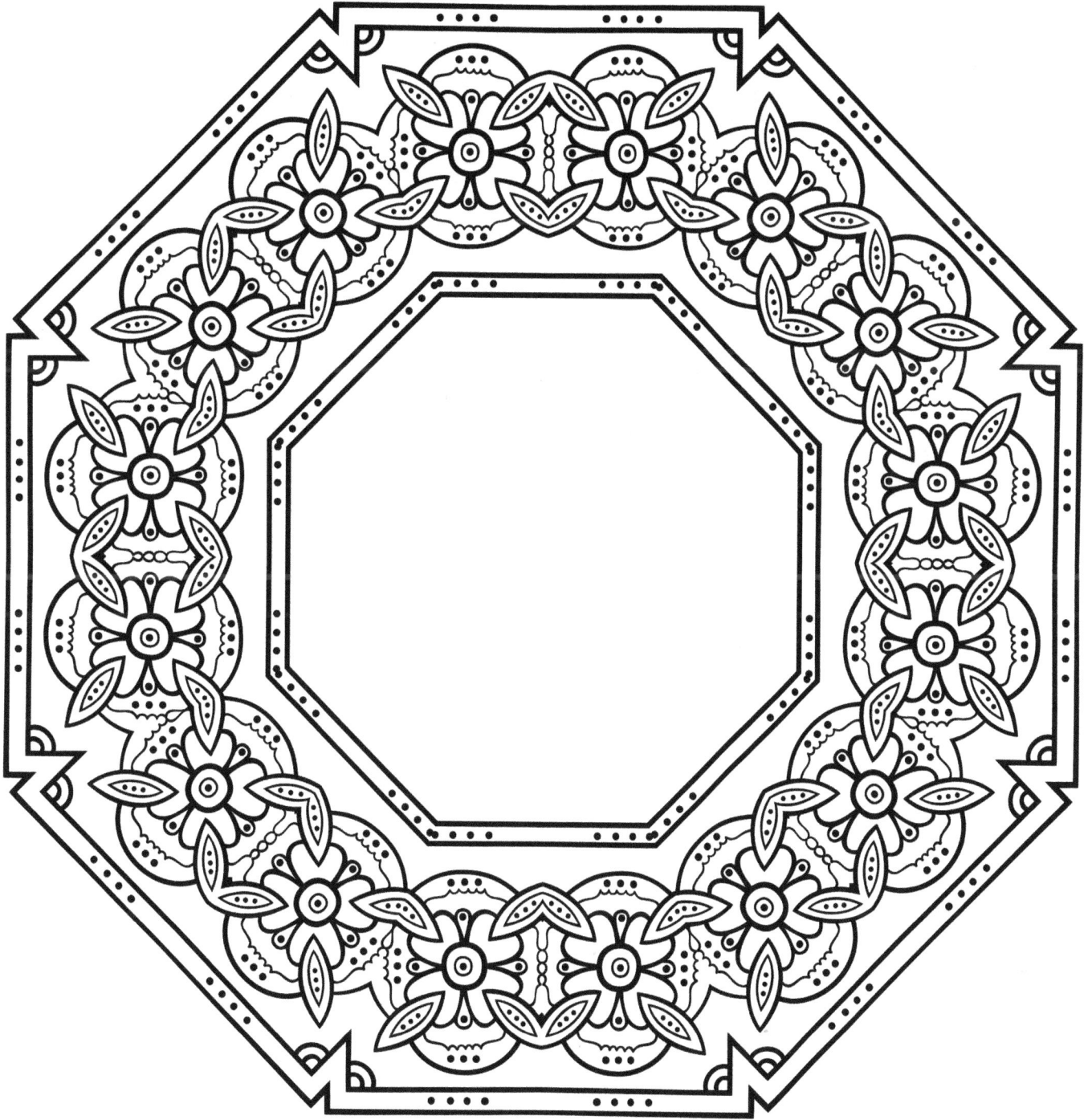

We relish news of our heroes, forgetting that we are extraordinary to somebody too.

Helen Hayes

When you have a dream, you've got to grab it and never let go.

Carol Burnett

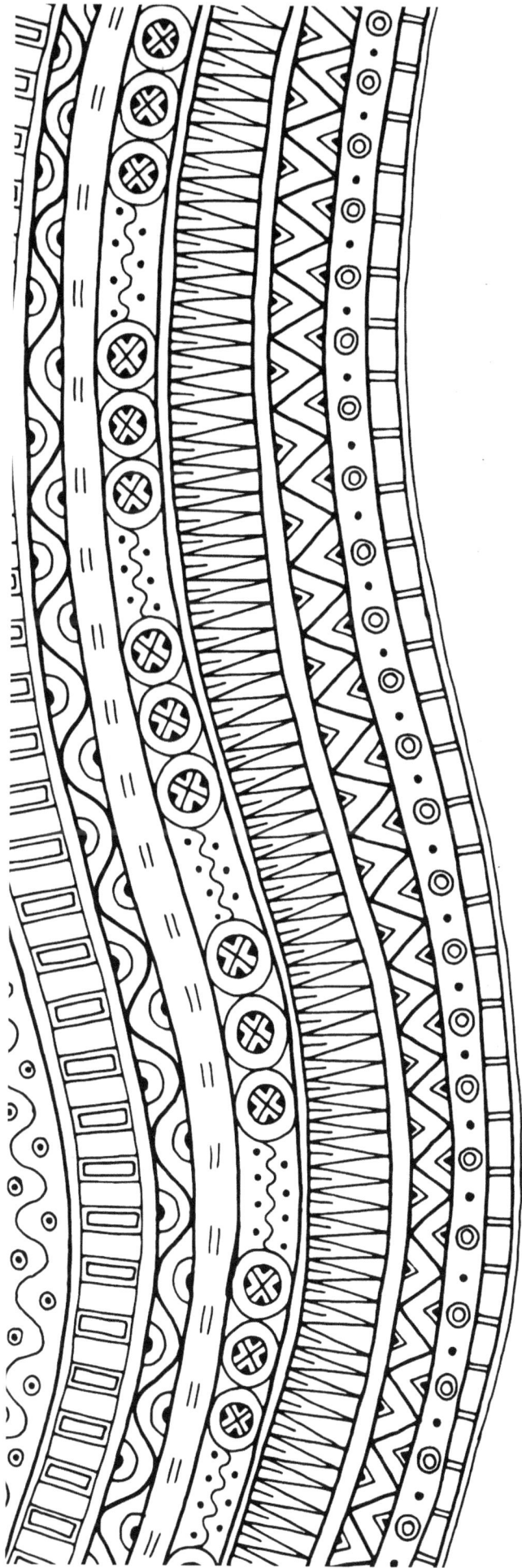

Great hopes make great men.

Thomas Fuller

Once I knew only darkness and stillness... my life was without past or future... but a little word from the fingers of another fell into my hand that clutched at emptiness, and my heart leaped to the rapture of living.

Helen Keller

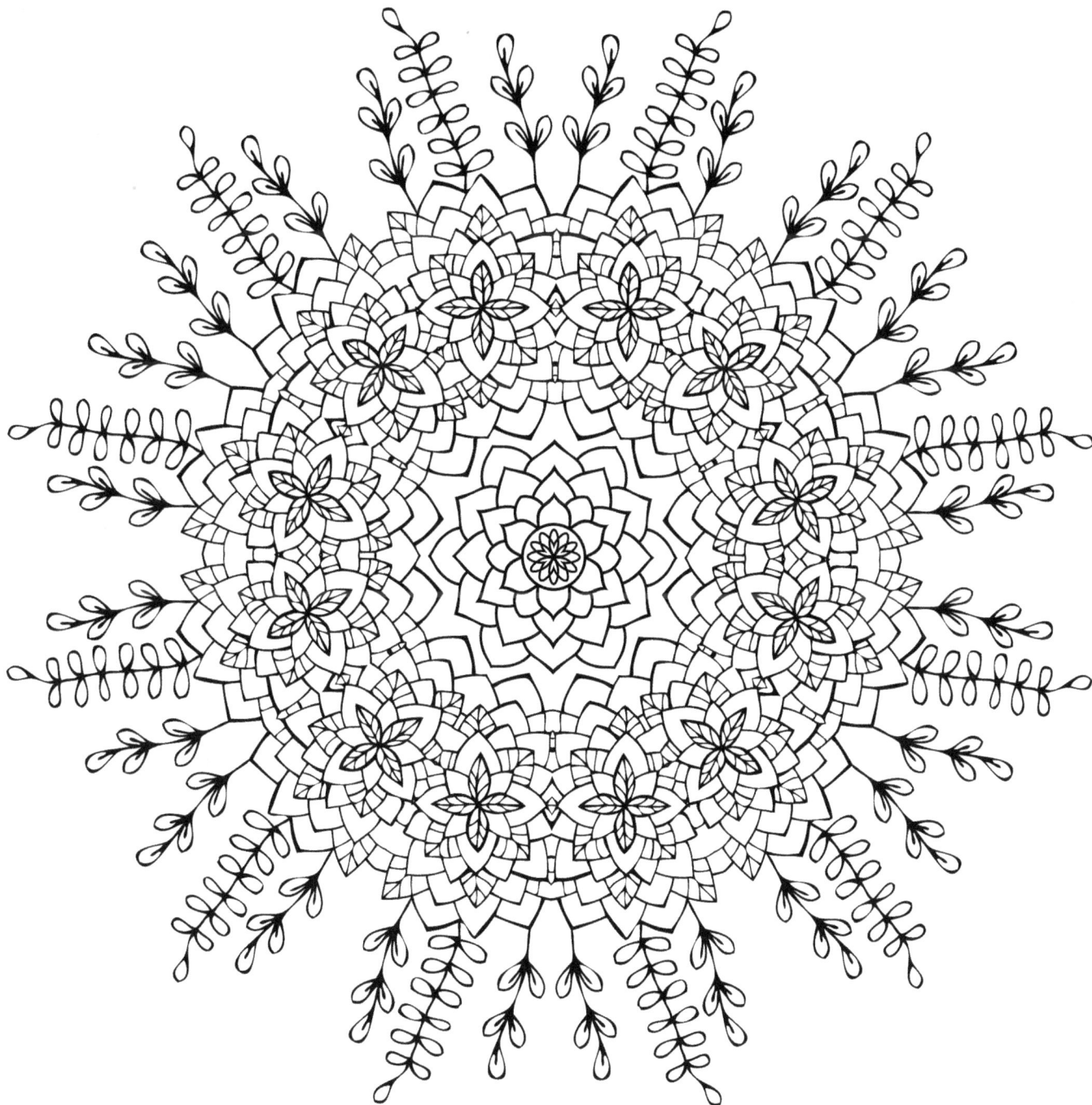

Each day provides its own gifts.

Marcus Aurelius

In oneself lies the whole world and if you know how to look and learn, the door is there and the key is in your hand. Nobody on earth can give you either the key or the door to open, except yourself.

Jiddu Krishnamurti

M

ost of us have far more courage than we ever dreamed we possessed.

Dale Carnegie

I've been absolutely terrified every moment of my life - and I've never let it keep me from doing a single thing I wanted to do.

Georgia O'Keeffe

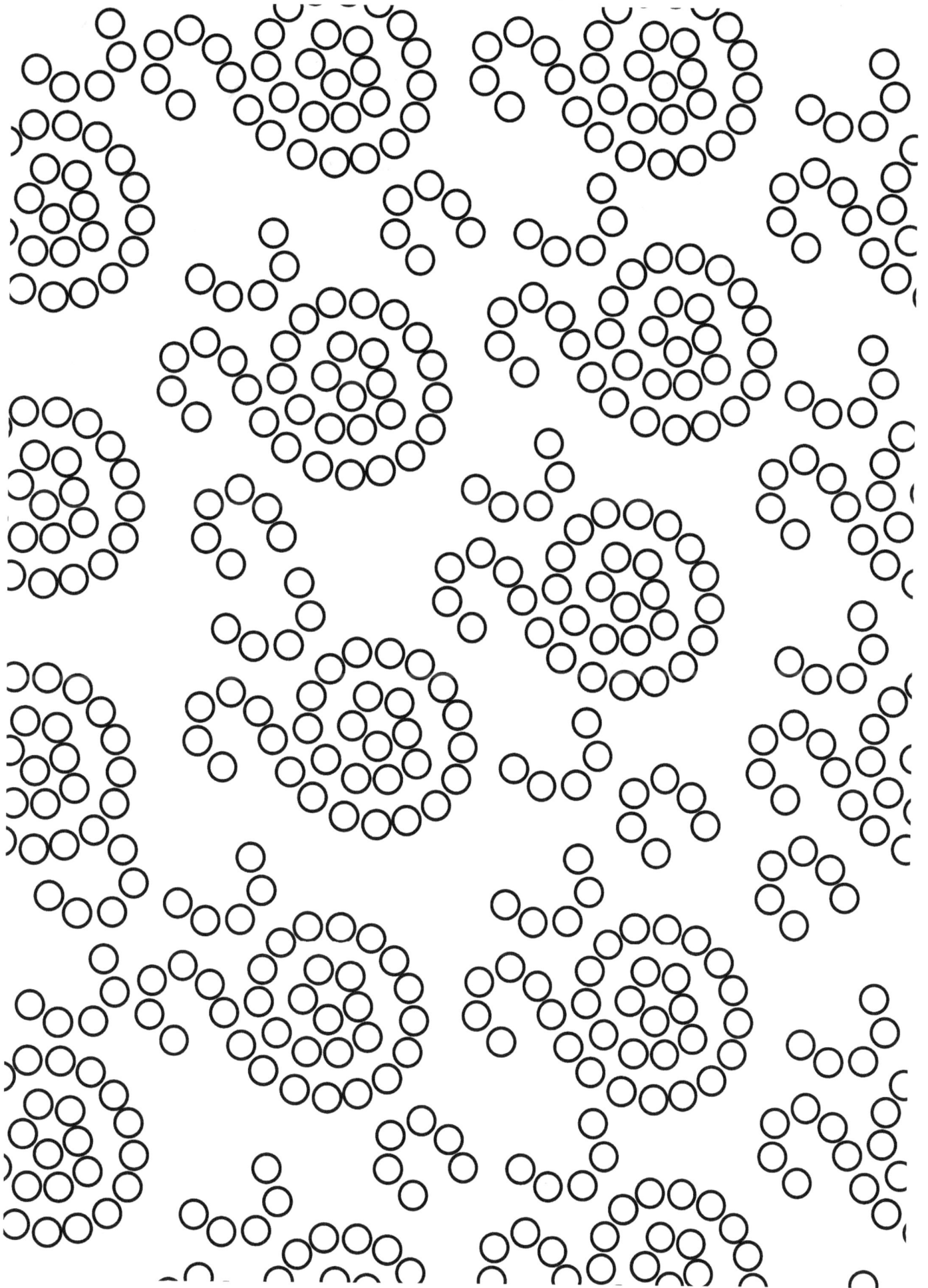

The essential elements of giving are power and love - activity and affection - and the consciousness of the race testifies that in the high and appropriate exercise of these is a blessedness greater than any other.

Mark Hopkins

Ideas shape the course of history.

John Maynard Keynes

For a gallant spirit there can never be defeat.

Wallis Simpson

There is nothing stronger in the
world than gentleness.

Han Suyin

Nothing is worth more than this day.

Johann Wolfgang von Goethe

And now, this is the sweetest and most glorious day that ever my eyes did see.

Donald Cargill

The power of imagination makes us infinite.

John Muir

I celebrate myself, and sing myself.

Walt Whitman

Grace is the beauty of form under the influence of freedom.

Friedrich Schiller

Our ideals are our better selves.

Amos Bronson Alcott

Nothing makes one feel so strong as a call for help.